LIFE IN CHRISTIAN
MOTHER GOOSE™
LAND

Volume III
of
the Trilogy

Library of Congress Catalog Card Number: 83-70989
ISBN 0-933724-13-6

Printed in the United States of America.

First Printing, July 1983

LIFE IN **CHRISTIAN MOTHER GOOSE**™ LAND

Paraphrased Text and Original Text
by
Marjorie Ainsborough Decker

Illustrated by
Theanna Sparr
Colleen Murphy Scott

Book Design
Marjorie Ainsborough Decker

GRUMPY HOLLOW

RAIN FOREST

POETREE DALE

NOTHING IS IMPOSSIBLE POSSUM

NOOKS & CRANNIES

GRANDPA MOLE'S HOUSE & HOLE

BROTHER RABBIT

POLLYWOGGLE

LUCY LADYBUG

COUSIN MOLE'S PEA PATCH

DANDELION SEA

BRIDGE LANDMARK

CHIPMUNK CHIGGER

DIPLEY DOCKERLEE

BLOSSOM BAY

DECKER PRESS, INC.
Publishers of Best-Seller Classics
GRAND JUNCTION, CO 81502

AFFECTIONATELY DEDICATED
TO
MY MOTHER
A CHAMPION STORYTELLER
IN HER OWN RIGHT
WHOSE
OVERCOMING JOY
SPIRIT AND COURAGE
IS THE
HERITAGE
SHE LEFT FOR US
AND FOR
ALL CHILDREN EVERYWHERE

STORYTELLER'S NOTE

"In Him was life; and the life was the light of men."

Spurgeon, years ago said: "A child of God should be a visible beatitude for joy and happiness, and a living doxology for gratitude and adoration."

The apostle Paul ringingly exhorts God's people to, "Rejoice in the Lord, alway."

From the Mustard Mountains, the Nooks and Crannies, the Rain Forest, Cobblers' Common, Grumpy Hollow and Polly-Woggle Park, the theme of rejoicing in God's love and goodness weaves in and out of the tapestry of tales in the third volume of the Christian Mother Goose Trilogy, *Life in Christian Mother Goose Land.*

The third book of the *Trilogy* is set around a single day in this mythical land, as quaint characters and creatures make their way to the annual Feast of Rejoicing at Dandelion Sea. The many foundational Bible themes, laced throughout the variety of rhymes and stories, are clothed in allegory and imagination; with the sure confidence that the timeless love of God is, in itself, the safest and most delightful place for a child's imagination and life to grow.

It is my hope that, in the happy nature of God's blessing, the *Christian Mother Goose Trilogy* will be used as a contributing tool, joining the many other varied instruments which daily mold and gently shape little lives to be conformed to the image of the Lord Jesus Christ; leading children ever onward and upward with the Christ of God who made them for Himself. And that children all around the world will stand with the Psalmist in breathing forth the most excellent Name of the Lord!–the ultimate anthem for which the gift of the breath of life was given.

With the *Christian Mother Goose Book*, the *Christian Mother Goose Treasury*, and *Life in Christian Mother Goose Land* now complete, the course of this Trilogy is set in harmony with tale-makers and tool-makers everywhere who make up that Armada of a rejoicing people who know their God, and who, with voices young and old, speak that "...living doxology of gratitude and adoration,"..."Let everything that hath breath praise the Lord!"

Marjorie Ainsborough Decker

OFF TO THE FEAST OF REJOICING!

"Hurray! Hurray! It's a new today!
My balloon is up and we're hoisting;
There's much to be done,
So get up with the sun,
And prepare for the Feast of Rejoicing!"

Up, up and away, without delay,
And with Grandpa Mole cheery-voicing,
The balloon so grand,
Sailed over the land
To announce the Feast of Rejoicing!

"Friends, bring good fare, for all to share
In God's love and goodness, together.
It's a day to enjoy,
Old or young, girl or boy,
Celebrate in the finest of weather!"

Grandpa Mole's loud shout very soon brought out
Humpty Dumpty, and Miss Muffet, too.
And Little Bo-Peep,
With all her sheep,
Ran to tell her friend, Little Boy Blue.

7

Mother Goose from the air, dropped everywhere,
The announcements of time and of place.
On every hillside
Windows popped open wide,
"Yes, we're coming!" called each cheery face.

"Now that's very nice," said the Three Kind Mice,
"We'll take cheese and we'll start out quite soon.
At the top of the hill,
We'll remind Jack and Jill
To be at the park by twelve, noon."

8

With rustle and bustle, and tussle and hustle,
Frogs, chipmunks and crickets and beavers,
With otters and moles,
Are leaving house-holes,
For the Feast of Rejoicing believers!

So, come little guest to the Feast with the rest,
You'll hear stories you'll quite understand;
Now open the book,
And listen and look
At the life in this wonderful land.

A BLESSING ON YOUR HEAD

A blessing on your head,
A blessing on your toe;
A blessing, little one,
To keep you safe
Where'er you go.

A blessing on your nose,
A blessing on your ears;
A blessing, little one,
To keep you happy
Through the years.

A blessing on your lips,
A blessing on your eyes;
A blessing, little one,
To help you grow
Like Jesus—wise!

A blessing on your hands,
A blessing on your days;
A blessing now
To bless the Lord,
With little hearts of praise!

RING-A-RING O' ROSES

Ring-a-ring o' roses,
  A pocket full of posies,
It's true! It's true!
  Jesus rose for me and you!

Ring-a-ring o' roses,
  A pocket full of posies,
It's true! It's true!
  He's coming back for me and you!

THREE LITTLE KITTENS

Three little kittens
　　Lost their mittens,
And they began to cry,
　　"Oh, mother dear,
　　We sadly fear
We lost our mittens nearby."

"Lost your mittens!
　　Then little kittens,
Take lamps and look, don't cry.
　　Sweep every nook,
　　And seek and look
For mittens, both low and high."

Three little kittens
　　Found their mittens,
And joyfully did cry,
　　"Oh, mother dear,
　　See here, see here!
Our mittens we found close by!"

"Found your mittens!
　　Good little kittens,
Bring all your friends for pie.
　　The lost is found!
　　We'll dance around!
Three little kittens and I."

12

LITTLE FISHY
IN THE BROOK

Little fishy in the brook,
   I can catch you quickly, look!
Bigger fishy in the lake,
   Needs more work for me to take.
Biggest fish down in the sea,
   Catching you takes two of me!
Great, strong fish down in the deep,
   Takes twelve boys to catch and keep!

DOWN A GRASSY BANK

Down a grassy bank
In the bright warm sun,
Lives a wise mother mouse
And her little mouse—
    ONE!
"LOVE," said the mother,
"I love," said the one;
So they lived in love
In the bright warm sun.

Down a grassy bank
Where the stream runs through,
Lives a wise mother fish
And her little fishes—
TWO!
"JOY!" said the mother,
"We've joy," said the two;
So they lived in joy
Where the stream runs through.

15

Down a grassy bank
In a willow tree,
Lives a wise mother dove
And her little doves—
　　　THREE!
"PEACE," said the mother,
"We've peace," said the three;
So they lived in peace
In the willow tree.

Down a grassy bank
Near the beavers' shore,
Lives a wise mother beaver
And her little beavers—
　　　FOUR!
"PATIENCE," said the mother,
"We've patience," said the four;
So they gnawed in patience
Near the beavers' shore.

Down a grassy bank
Where the otters dive,
Lives a wise mother otter
And her little otters—
      FIVE!
"KINDNESS," said the mother,
"We've kindness," said the five;
So they played in kindness
Where the otters dive.

Down a grassy bank
Where the acorns mix,
Lives a wise mother squirrel
And her little squirrels—
      SIX!
"GOODNESS," said the mother,
"We've goodness," said the six;
So they shared in goodness
Where the acorns mix.

Down a grassy bank
Looking up to Heaven,
Lives a wise mother frog
And her little frogs—
      SEVEN!
"FAITH!" said the mother,
"We've faith," said the seven;
So they jumped in faith
Looking up to Heaven.

Down a grassy bank
Where the ducklings skate,
Lives a wise mother duck
And her little ducklings—
      EIGHT!
"GENTLE," said the mother,
"We're gentle," said the eight;
So they were most gentle
Where the ducklings skate.

Down a grassy bank
Where the rabbits dine,
Lives a wise mother rabbit
And her little rabbits—
          NINE!
"CONTROL!" said the mother,
"We've control," said the nine;
So they nibbled in control
Where the rabbits dine.

COCK ROBIN GOT UP EARLY

Cock Robin got up early,
    On baby's first birthday,
And flew to baby's house
    To sing a happy roundelay:
"Precious little baby,
    Jesus loves you dear;
Grow to be more like Him,
    As I return each year."

KNOCK AT THE DOOR

Knock at the door,
Peep in.
Lift up the latch,
Walk in!
Welcome, dear Lord!
Join in.
Lift up our hands,
Praise Him!

RAIN, RAIN, GO AWAY

Rain, rain, go away,
　Come again another day.
Cloud, cloud, like a hand,
　Rain again across the land.

I LOVE LITTLE PUSSY

I love little pussy,
　Her coat is so warm,
And if I don't hurt her
　She'll do me no harm.
So I'll not pull her tail
　Nor drive her away,
But pussy and I
　Very gently will play.

21

LITTLE POLLY FLINDERS

Little Polly Flinders,
    Knows a word that hinders;
Instead of "might,"
    She says, "Must, must, must!"
Another word is "doubt,"
    Which she just turns roundabout,
And cheerily says,
    "I will trust, trust, trust!"

SOMEBODY!

A little knock came quietly.
They said, "Don't look,
It's *nobody*."
But I thought it was
Somebody!
And so I looked,
Because, you see,
God did not make a
Nobody!
He makes a special
Somebody!
He makes a special
You and *me!*
And so I looked;
I looked, you see,
To see that special
Somebody!

I FILLED A LITTLE BASKET

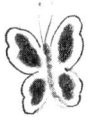

I filled a little basket
  With some cherries from a tree;
I filled a little box
  With some shells along the sea;
I filled a little bag
  With some speckled rocks I found;
I filled a little hole
  With some soil piled on the ground;

I filled my little mouth
  With some happy songs to God;
I filled my little hands
  With His kindly Shepherd's rod;
I filled my little ears
  With His Words, to guide my feet;
Then *He* filled little *me*,
  With His love and Spirit, sweet.

THIS IS THE WAY

This is the way the fathers ride,
  "Emmanuel! Praise the Lord!"

This is the way the mothers ride,
  "Bread of Life! Praise the Lord!"

This is the way the children ride,
  "Precious Jesus! Praise the Lord!"

This is the way the grandpas ride,
  "Counsellor! Praise the Lord!"

This is the way the grandmas ride,
  "Comforter! Praise the Lord!"

This is the way the young men ride,
  "Lion of Judah! Praise the Lord!"

This is the way the ladies ride,
  "Rose of Sharon! Praise the Lord!"

This is the way the uncles ride,
  "Prince of Peace! Praise the Lord."

This is the way the aunties ride,
  "Living Word! Praise the Lord!"

Fathers, mothers, sisters, brothers,
  Know these Names, and many others;
But, returning home, they'll sing,
  "Lord of Lords, and King of Kings!"

THE BEST TOUCH OF ALL!

I love to touch my rabbit's nose,
   I love to touch a silky rose;
I love to touch my pony's mane,
   I love to touch a showery rain;
I love to touch my cushion chair,
   I love to touch my teddy bear;
I love to touch my new boots' leather,
   I love to touch my peacock feather;
I love to touch my little sail,
   I love to touch my puppy's tail;
I love to touch my big red ball,
   But there's a touch that's best of all!...

When Mommy and Daddy touch me!

COUSIN MOLES—
THE TIME THIEVES

Tilly, Tolly and Dolly,
  With Toggle Mole, as well,
Noggin, Mogie and Rimpy Mole,
  Are hurrying, you can tell.

Seven little Cousin Moles,
  As chipper as can be,
Are riding off to wake the town
  Of Dippley Dockerlee.

They want to make the Feast Day
  Last longer—if they can;
So they got up very early
  To carry out their plan.

They rode past Grandpa Mole's house,
  And Polly-Woggle Park,
Through Dandelion Sea's green lanes,
  To reach the bridge landmark.

Pedalling hard across the bridge,
  Through fields of four-o'clocks,
At last they came to the village
  Where everything goes, "Tick-Tock."

26

In Dippley Dockerlee, you see,
    Are flocks and flocks and flocks,
Of roly-poly Docker Bugs
    Who look like little clocks.

The Docker Bugs are careful
    To redeem the time each day;
They work and praise while letting,
    "Yea" be "Yea," and "Nay" be "Nay!"

The clockmaker in the village
    Checks the sundial twice a day;
And four-o'clock flowers open,
    Keeping time in *their* own way.

A music clock in the Tower
    Booms each hour, a mighty "BONG!"
And at eight o'clock each morning
    It plays the town's theme song:

"Docker Bugs, we're Docker Bugs,
Roly-poly Docker Bugs,
As we roly right along,
'Praise The Lord!'
That is our song.
We redeem the time each day,
'Yea' is 'Yea,' and 'Nay' is 'Nay',
But there's always time to say,
'Praise The Lord!'
The Docker Way."

27

Now, Cousin Moles rode into town
   As Docker Bugs still slept;
In summertime they sleep outdoors,
   So Cousin Moles softly crept.

"We're going to turn their clocks back,"
   Toggle Mole said, "so that we
Can make a happy, *longer* day
   For Dippley Dockerlee!"

So, one by one, they turned back
   All the clocks, from six to four;
And changed the Tower clock
   Between the "Tick-Tock" of each snore.

Then Cousin Moles departed,
　　And left the town in bed,
Not knowing they were being watched
　　From high up overhead!

For Grandpa Mole and Mother Goose
　　Had watched the whole affair,
While dropping invitations
　　To the Feast, from in mid-air.

"Now, what are Cousin Moles up to?"
　　Grandpa Mole asked curiously;
"I think since all our work is done,
　　I'll drop you off and see."

At Mother Goose's cottage,
　　Grandpa Mole came gently down,
"Your own front door, dear Mother Goose,
　　As soft as eider-down!"

"I'll meet you later at the Feast;
　　I'm bringing two young friends,"
Mother Goose said. "Off you go!
　　To help Moles make amends."

Now…Docker Bugs get up at six,
    And start the day with song;
But they had overslept two hours
    When the Tower clock rang "BONG!"

Soon everyone was busy
    In the things that make up days;
Yet in all their busy moments
    They did not forget to Praise!

The old clockmaker on his way
    To open shop at nine,
Picked a bunch of four-o'clocks,
    And checked the sundial's time.

The sundial's shadow pointed to
    Almost eleven o'clock;
"How can that be? Just look at me!"
    He gasped in "tick-tock" shock.

He hurried to the Tower clock;
    Mayor Dippley Dock was there,
Arranging for a big parade
    Around the market square.

"Mayor Dippley Dock, we've lost two hours.
    Someone has stolen time!
The sundial shows eleven o'clock,
    And Docker Bugs show nine!"

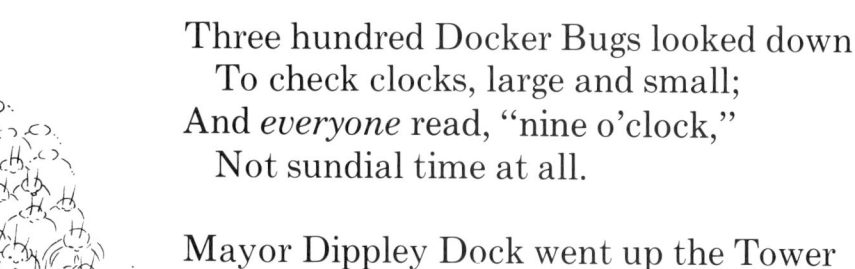

Three hundred Docker Bugs looked down
    To check clocks, large and small;
And *everyone* read, "nine o'clock,"
    Not sundial time at all.

Mayor Dippley Dock went up the Tower
    And called to his parade,
"Someone has stolen two hours time;
    A 'Time-thief' escapade!"

"They've tampered with our Docker clocks,
    But the one clock they forgot,
Is God's big sun! So Praise the Lord!
    We know their 'Time-thief' plot."

"The hours we've lost call for a change,
    We must cancel our parade;
'Dockers For Soccer' will have to wait,
    It's time for our work and trade."

With disappointed faces,
    And knowing they must hurry,
The Docker Bugs re-set their clocks,
    With fussing, fret and scurry.

Mayor Dippley Dock cried, "Dockers!
    We *redeem* the time each day;
If we react in blame and fault,
    We'll waste *more* time away."

"Our time may have been stolen,
    But good humor we must keep;
Right now, let's all forgive the thieves,
    Then *extra* time we'll reap!"

31

Meanwhile, to celebrate the Feast,
   Cousin Moles were gathering peas,
When Grandpa Mole walked through the patch
   And said, "Attention, please!"

"A certain situation,
   In Dippley Dockerlee,
Regarding time on Docker clocks,
   May cause an emergency."

"Emergency!" squeaked Cousin Moles,
   With voices in dismay;
"Dear Grandpa Mole, we only meant
   To give them a longer day."

Grandpa Mole leaned forward,
   And Cousin Moles grew red;
"I'm sure the Docker Bugs will all
   Forgive you," Grandpa said.

So Tilly, Tolly, Dolly,
  And Toggle Mole at rear;
With Noggin, Mogie, Rimpy Mole,
  All pedalling in high gear,
Rode back to say, "We're sorry,"
  To Dippley Dockerlee;
Then seven little Cousin Moles
  Came home so happily!

A FAMILY

Who ever could have thought of it?
A little house with room to fit
A Mommy-mom and Daddy-dad,
With boys and girls
To make them glad!
Could *you* have ever thought of it?
I never could, I do admit.
What lovely plans *GOD* must have knit,
For *HE'S* the One who thought of it—
    A FAMILY!

MONDAY'S CHILD

Monday's child will seek God's face,
Tuesday's child is full of grace,
Wednesday's child in faith will grow,
Thursday's child God's love will show,
Friday's child is loving and giving,
Saturday's child thanks God for living,
And the child that is born
On the Lord's first day,
Will trust Him as He leads the way.

35

THE FIVE COBBLERS

Over the hill from Dandelion Sea,
And just two hundred hops
From the bingleberry hedge,
Is a little vale called
Cobblers' Common.
It sits at the foot of
The Mustard Mountains.

Five clever cobblers live there.
Their names, Cobblecut, Stitchtight,
Nailtap, Buffkin and Stampen have
Been passed down for hundreds of
Years in the cobbler family.

Their cobblestone workshop nestles
In the cedar trees, where the path
Begins that leads over
The Mustard Mountains.

Every pair of shoes
The five cobblers make,
Are carefully crafted
For the many travelers
Who go on the long journey
Across the high Mustard Mountains.

Curiously, all the shoes are stamped
According to an old scroll,
Hanging in the workshop, which reads:

"Cobbler family, in this vale,
You are part of a wondrous tale.
In your calling you will find
Shoes to make of every kind,
Since the ones who pass this way
Will need your craft from day to day.
Make each pair with skill—and strong!
Bless them with The Cobbler's Song;
Stamp the Great Seal on every sole,
Thus keep the words of the
    Cobbler's Scroll."

As they were faithful cobblers—
Cobblecut cut...
    Stitchtight stitched...
        Nailtap nailed...
            Buffkin buffed...
And Stampen stamped every
Sole with the Great Seal
Bearing The Cobbler's Song.

38

Sadly, there was only one line left
Of The Cobbler's Song.
The great seal had gradually worn away
With much use, and all that could be
Read these days were the words,
   "How lovely on the mountains…"

Of course, the great-grandfather cobblers,
Many years ago, had known every
Jot and tittle of The Cobbler's Song.
But word by word
It had slowly faded away.

Nevertheless, the five little cobblers
Faithfully sang the one line left
On The Great Seal,
"How lovely on the mountains…"
Over every pair of shoes they made
To go over the Mustard Mountains.

They were happy to work hard
Making shoes, year after year;
All shapes and sizes,
For all kinds of travelers
Who gladly came to their
Cobblestone workshop.

Some came for two shoes,
  A few inches long;
Some came for four shoes
  To last a life long.
Some came for sandals
  Made from the best leather;
Some came for boots that would
  Stand the worst weather.
Some wanted low shoes,
  And some wanted high.
Some wanted buckles,
  And some, a lace tie.
Some wanted black shoes,
  And some wanted red.
Some wanted brown shoes,
  And some, green instead…

But they *all* wanted to walk over the Mustard Mountains!

One day Stampen said,

"Why do the travelers
   Continue to climb
Up the Mustard Mountains,
   Time after time?
What is their purpose?
   What do they do?
And what is our part
   In making each shoe?
Let's make 'travelers shoes'
   For ourselves, and find out
What The Cobbler's Song
   Is all about."

"I'll gladly cut shoes for that
   Very purpose," said Cobblecut...
"I'll gladly stitch shoes for that
   Very purpose," said Stitchtight...
"I'll gladly nail shoes for that
   Very purpose," said Nailtap...
"I'll gladly buff shoes for that
   Very purpose," said Buffkin...
"And I'll gladly stamp the Great Seal
   On the shoes that will take us over
   The Mustard Mountains," said Stampen.
And they all shook hands on their promise.

41

With cheerful hurry-scurry,
　The cobbling fast began,
As the little cobblers cobbled
　Handsome shoes, to perfect plan.

Cobblecut's were tinted blue;
　Stitchtight's brown with stringing;
Nailtap's green, and Buffkin's gold,
　And Stampen's red, with fringing.

When Stampen stamped the new shoes,
　They sang The Cobbler's Song,
"How lovely on the mountains…"
　Seven times, to make it long.

Bright, early in the morning,
　They marched off up the glen,
Singing in their special shoes;
　Determined little men.

Up, up the rocky pathway,
　And past the waterfall;
Through clumps of swaying bluebells,
　And through the pine trees tall.

Far up the Mustard Mountains,
　And marching at their best,
Five weary little cobblers said,
　"It's time to stop and rest."

And there, just off the pathway,
  A small rock shelter stood.
"Welcome Travelers, Rest and Dine,"
  Said a sign made out of wood.

Water bubbled from a spring,
  With mugs in good supply;
And bread and cheese in baskets
  On a polished stump nearby.

All five cobblers bowed their heads,
  To thank God for this care;
And as they ate the good food,
  They heard singing in the air…

"How lovely on the mountains
  Are the Good News feet,
Bringing happy tidings
  Of peace to all they meet…"

"The Cobbler's Song," they whispered,
  "How wondrous are those words.
Where is the music coming from?
  The trees?—the wind?—the birds?"

So once again they set out,
  Then stopped in great surprise,
For as they passed the Whistling Caves,
  A whistling song did arise!

43

"How lovely on the mountains
    Are the Good News feet,
Bringing happy tidings
    Of peace to all they meet.
Feet so quick to climb
    With the Good, Good News,
Helped along by cobblers
    Who make the Good News shoes…

"That's more of The Cobbler's Song,"
    Five voices whispered low,
Peering down the craggy caves
    Where the song disappeared below.

With staffs in hand, the cobblers
    Trudged up Cathedral Heights;
"The top!" they cried. "We've reached it!
    Then gasped at the dazzling sight.

A sunny world lay dancing
    Over miles of gold and green;
Flowers tinkling, breezes singing
    With voices of choirs, unseen.

A host of waving banners
    Flew from cottage roofs around.
Good News rang out everywhere;
    The peaks were alive with sound!

The cobblers' hearts all jumped for joy
    At the singing, happy sight;
And best of all, The Cobbler's Song
    They heard—with power and might!

44

They listened well, and learned it,
　　As seeking cobblers ought,
And praised God for the Good News
　　The faithful travelers had brought.

　　"Let's hurry to the workshop,"
　　　Each cobbler soon agreed,
　　"And carve back in the Great Seal
　　　The *whole* song for all to read."

　　Quickly they ran, descending
　　　The path to their little vale;
　　Knowing now their happy part
　　　In the old scroll's "wondrous tale."

So if you pass their workshop
　　On the day they're making shoes,
You can hear The Cobbler's Song,
　　And learn the GOOD, GOOD NEWS from...
　　Cobblecut, Stitchtight, Nailtap
　　　Buffkin and Stampen...
　　"How lovely on the mountains
　　　Are the Good News feet,
Bringing happy tidings
　　Of peace to all they meet.
Feet so quick to climb
　　With the Good, Good News,
Helped along by cobblers
　　Who make the Good News shoes;
Publishing salvation
　　Across the mountain chains,
Feet are bringing Good News!...
　　OUR GOD REIGNS!"

45

A LITTLE BEE
SAT ON A WALL

A little bee sat on a wall.
"Buzz," said he,
And that was all.
But then I listened carefully
He "Buzzed" again,
And said to me,
"God loves you, little one."

A little bird sat on a twig.
"Chirp," said he,
(Not very big).
But then I listened carefully,
He "Chirped" again,
And said to me,
"God loves you, little one."

46

A little frog sat on a stone.
"Croak," said he,
Just once—alone.
But then I listened carefully,
He "Croaked " again,
And said to me,
"God loves you, little one."

A little owl sat in an oak.
"Whoo," said he,
That's all he spoke.
But then I listened carefully,
He "Whoo-ed " again,
And said to me,
"God loves you, little one."

47

WHERE ARE YOU GOING TO, MY PRETTY MAID?

"Where are you going to,
  My pretty maid?"
"I'm going a-listening,
  Sir," she said.

"May I go with you,
  My pretty maid?"
"You're kindly welcome,
  Sir," she said.

"What will we listen to,
  My pretty maid?"
"My Father's good Words,
  Kind sir," she said.

"Where will we listen,
  My pretty maid?"
"Within Father's house,
  Kind sir," she said.

"How will we listen,
   My pretty maid?"
"With all of our heart,
   Kind sir," she said.

"Who is your Father,
   My pretty maid?"
"The Lord God in Heaven,
   Kind sir," she said.

"How can we reach Him,
   My pretty maid?"
"I'll show you the Way,
   Kind sir," she said.

"Jesus, The Way, The Truth
   And The Life,
Will lead you to Him,
   Kind sir," she said.

FROM WIBBLETON TO WOBBLETON

From Wibbleton to Wobbleton,
  A bridge lies in between;
From Wobbleton to Wibbleton,
  The same bridge can be seen.

From Wibbleton to Wobbleton
  Folk start their journey singing;
From Wibbleton to Wobbleton,
  Across the bridge a-ringing!

From Wobbleton to Wibbleton,
  Folk start their journey cringing;
From Wobbleton to Wibbleton,
  Across the bridge a-clinging.

50

From Wibbleton to Wobbleton,
  They cross the bridge robust;
From Wibbleton to Wobbleton,
  Across the bridge in trust!

From Wobbleton to Wibbleton,
  They tremble to start out;
From Wobbleton to Wibbleton,
  Across the bridge in doubt.

From Wibbleton to Wobbleton,
  They very soon get there;
From Wibbleton to Wobbleton,
  Across the bridge in prayer!

From Wobbleton to Wibbleton,
  They cannot stride or hurry;
From Wobbleton to Wibbleton,
  Across the bridge in worry.

From Wibbleton to Wobbleton,
  The bridge is safe and sound;
From Wobbleton to Wibbleton,
  The same bridge can be found!

So, would you live in Wibbleton?
  Or would you live in Wobbleton?
The bridge will give the answer
  When you cross some day.

51

YOU MADE THE MONTHS
FOR ME

JANUARY brings the snow,
    Makes our feet
And fingers glow;
    Gentle Jesus,
Then I know,
    You made the snow for me.

FEBRUARY brings the rain,
    Thaws the frozen
Lakes again;
    Gentle Jesus,
It is plain,
    You made the rain for me.

MARCH brings breezes,
    Loud and shrill,
Stirs the dancing daffodil;
    Gentle Jesus,
All to please,
    You made the breeze for me.

APRIL brings the primrose sweet,
  Scatters daisies
At our feet;
  Gentle Jesus,
Speak the hours,
  You made the flowers for me.

MAY brings flocks of pretty lambs,
  Skipping by
Their fleecy dams;
  Gentle Jesus,
Then I see,
  You made the lambs for me.

JUNE brings perfumed,
  Velvet roses,
Fills the children's
  Hands with posies;
Gentle Jesus,
  My heart knows,
You made the rose for me.

53

Hot JULY brings
  Cooling showers,
Apricots and gillyflowers;
  Gentle Jesus,
By your powers,
  You made the showers for me.

AUGUST brings the sheaves of corn,
  Then the harvest
Home is borne,
  Gentle Jesus,
I believe,
  You made the sheaves for me.

Warm SEPTEMBER brings the fruit,
  Festivals with
Harp and flute;
  Gentle Jesus,
I salute,
  You made the fruit for me.

54

Fresh OCTOBER brings the pheasant,
　　Then to gather nuts
Is pleasant;
　　Gentle Jesus,
Always present,
　　You made the pheasant for me.

Gray NOVEMBER brings bare trees,
　　Crackling leaves
Up to our knees;
　　Gentle Jesus,
I perceive,
　　You made the leaves for me.

Chill DECEMBER brings us home,
　　Blazing fire
At evening's gloom;
　　Gentle Jesus,
Though I roam,
　　You made the home for me.

THE CHIMNEY SWEEP FLIGHT

Cousin Moles were off again
  To Polly-Woggle Park,
When over Chipmunk Chigger
  They saw something rather dark.

It kept growing in the sky,
  Puffing blacker—puffing bigger;
Noggin Mole cried, "Chimneys must be
  Blocked in Chipmunk Chigger!"

"I'm *sure* they're blocked," said Mogie,
  And Tilly nodded, too;
Tolly, Rimpy, Dolly,
  All agreed that was *their* view.

Toggle Mole, excitedly,
  Said, "Send out the alarm!
Send S.O.S. for chimney sweeps,
  Before that cloud does harm!"

Then Noggin got excited,
  "We're turning round," he cried;
"We'll all be heroes!" Toggle cheered,
  "The honors we'll divide."

"S.O.S," they shouted,
  Racing past each house and tree,
And caught the quick attention
  Of Benjamin Bumblebee.

56

Benjamin flew down swiftly,
  Buzzing over Noggin's head,
"What's all the shouting for?
  And the S.O.S.?" he said.

"We're rushing back to town,
  To get help for Chipmunk Chigger,
Their chimney flues are blocked,
  And the smoke-cloud's getting bigger!"

"Action! We need action!"
  Seven Cousin Moles cried out.
"I'll fly ahead," said Benjamin,
  "And warn the town, throughout."

"Hear ye, hear ye, hear ye!"
  Benjamin Bumblebee buzzed loud,
And soon in Dandelion Sea,
  He drew a startled crowd.

"Cousin Moles have seen a cloud,
  As black, as black as night;
Shutting all the sunshine out
  From Chipmunk Chiggerites."

Grandpa Mole and Brother Rabbit
  Both came hurrying in,
Along with Charlie Cricket,
  Who all questioned Benjamin.

"Cousin Moles alerted me,
  That black cloud's like a cloak;
Through chimney flues that must be cleaned,
  To conquer all that smoke."

Grandpa Mole spoke to the crowd,
　　With words right from his heart,
"Today's the Feast, but there's a job
　　To do! Who'll make a start?"

"I will! I'll help! I'm coming!"
　　Cried one, and then a dozen.
"We're coming, too!" And with those words,
　　Arrived the Moles—each Cousin.

"Come with me, young Cousin Moles,
　　You'll find great satisfaction,
In watching Dandelion Sea
　　Go quickly into action!"

"Oh, Grandpa Mole, we're ready
　　To fly off in your balloon!"
Cousin Moles jumped round and squeaked,
　　"We're a chimney sweep platoon!"

With brushes, brooms and buckets,
　　Feather dusters, rakes and mops,
A clean-up squad soon rallied round,
　　With multi-clean-up props.

"All hands on deck for rescue!"
　　Came Brother Rabbit's voice;
"Though we may miss the Feast Day,
　　We'll work and *still* rejoice!"

"It's written, whatsoever
　　That we do, we do with might;
Take off with prayer and purpose,
　　To remove that black-cloud blight."

Charlie launched the *Sharing Ship*,
　　All loaded down, and tooting;
With little rafts behind him,
　　To the rescue, all commuting.

58

Dressed in chimney sweep tall hats,
   With brushes standing by,
Grandpa Mole and Cousin Moles
   Flew on across the sky.

And there it was before them!
   A quivering, black-blob sight;
Noggin said, "See, Grandpa Mole?
   We all were right! Were right!"

"I'm going to drop," cried Grandpa Mole,
   "Hold on, mole girls and boys!"
But suddenly the cloud broke up,
   With humming, buzzing noise!

It broke in tiny pieces,
   And, what's more, the black cloud spoke!
"Greetings! Greetings! mole balloon,"
   Without a trace of smoke!

59

"Buzzing bees; they're buzzing bees!"
    Cried Cousin Moles, all red.
"Not 'buzzing bees,' we're 'Blessing Bees,'"
    The Queen Bee brightly said.

"We heard that Chipmunk Chigger
    Had no honey for each home.
We're here to bless this little town
    With plans of honeycomb."

Grandpa Mole then spoke right up,
    "Indeed, I'm quite relieved,
To find that Chipmunk Chigger's
    Not smoked out, as we believed."

"Goodbye, good moles. Goodbye, balloon.
    We must be off and working."
The bees flew off, but Cousin Moles
    Crouched in the basket, lurking.

Grandpa Mole laughed as he turned
    The big balloon around,
"You might as well stand up," said he,
    "And tell our friends on ground."

60

"Tell them what the black cloud was?"
  The Cousin Moles all mumbled.
"Of course, and they will all be glad
  Our Feast Day hasn't crumbled."

  "The Feast! The Feast! We'll be on time!
    Everyone still can go,"
  Happily shouted seven moles;
    "Good News! to all below."

  "Turn back, turn back, it's false alarm!
    No danger, in the least;
  We're still all clean; we're still on time,
    To celebrate the Feast!"

The *Sharing Ship* and all the rafts,
  "Toot-tooted," merrily,
As mops and pails turned homeward sails
  To Dandelion Sea.

When Cousin Moles had landed home,
  (No longer chimney-hatters)
Grandpa Mole said, "Little tongues
  Can kindle such great matters."

"We've learned our lesson, Grandpa Mole,
  'Be *sure* before you tell!' "
They blew a kiss, and Grandpa smiled,
  "All's well that ends so well."

61

I THINK GOD LIKES EVERY KIND OF SONG

I think God likes
  Every kind of song:
Every-kind-of-praise song,
  Old-or-nowadays song;
Kneeling-down-devout songs,
  Stomp-along-and-shout songs;
Hushy-quiet-soft-songs,
  Hats-all-on-or-off songs;
Sing-with-all-your-might songs,
  Dainty-sound-polite songs;
Whispered-little-prayer songs,
  Rocking-in-the-chair songs;
I think God likes
  Every kind of praise.

I think God likes
    Every kind of praise:
Hurry-fast-along-songs,
    Take-a-long-time-long songs;
Leave-the-third-verse-out songs,
    Can't-sing-it-without songs;
Barely-can-be-heard songs,
    All-alone-or-shared songs;
Big-cathedral-choir songs,
    Sitting-by-the-fire songs;
Little-bits-of-snatch songs,
    Concerts-by-the-batch songs;
I think God likes
    Every kind of song!

SIX LITTLE MICE SAT DOWN TO SPIN

Six little mice
Sat down to spin,
Six little days
To work therein.

One day for spinning…
    The wheel went, "Plack, Plack,"
One day for weaving…
    The loom went, "Clack, Clack,"
One day for cutting…
    With scissors, "Snip, Snip,"
One day for sewing…
    With needles, "Nip, Nip,"
One day for fitting…
    The mice cried, "OO-OO!"
One day for pressing…
    With irons, "Scoo, Scoo."

Six little mice
Sat down to spin,
Six little days
To work therein.

Six little mice dressed in cotton and cord,
Finished in time for the day of the Lord!

IS ANYBODY LISTENING?

Is anybody listening,
Listening, listening?
Is anybody listening,
Listening to me?
I saw a mouse
Stand on his head!
I saw a butterfly—
All red!
I ran home fast to tell
All that there was to see.

But no one even stopped and said,
  "You saw a *mouse*
  Stand on his head!
  You saw a *butterfly*—
  All red!
  What marvelous things
  You just have said!"
Instead, I just went up to bed,
And told it all to me!
Is anybody listening,
Listening, listening?
Is anybody listening,
Listening to me?

I disappeared
Inside my bed;
All you could see
Was just my head;
I closed my ears so tight
No sound could reach in me.

But though I shut the sound all out,
A little voice
Began to sprout
Inside myself,
And rose about
With words, just like
A waterspout
That swished and swirled
All round about,
As plain, as plain could be:
"Is anybody listening?
Listening, listening?
Is anybody listening,
Listening to ME?"

"*I* saw the mouse
Stand on his head;
I saw the butterfly—
All red!
I saw you run to tell
All that there was to see.
And when you hid inside your bed,
I whispered in your ear and said,
'Let all the little children
Come and talk to ME!'
For I am *always* listening,
Listening, listening;
I am *always* listening,
Listening carefully."

67

GRUMPY HOLLOW

Walking north of Dandelion Sea,
You pass Badger Burrows and follow
  A sign on the path,
    That says, "CAUTION! DON'T LAUGH—
YOU'RE NOW ENTERING GRUMPY HOLLOW."

A blue-green mist swirls through the trees
Of grumpwood, and moss-tangled bark;
  The Grumps live there,
    But they never share
In the Feast at Polly-Woggle Park.

68

They never come out to make new friends
With the rest of the countryside;
   They don't like the sun,
   Or words such as "fun,"
Their vocabulary's not very wide.

It mainly consists of words like, "grump,"
"Crabapple," and "bitter," or "sour."
   "Gloomy" and "glum,"
   "Complain" and "humdrum,"
They practice these words by the hour.

At last here's the day all have waited for,
And the Grumps are gathering together;
   Dr. Frump is the Chief,
   And grumps through his teeth,
"No doubt, we'll have gloomy-glum weather."

"Now, Grumps, as you know, today is the Feast,
The Feast of Grumbling, no less;
   As your usual host,
   I suggest make the most
Of your worries and general distress."

"We'll start with our song, then follow along
With a game of croquet, as we do;
   The song has no key,
   But try following me,
You can struggle, the pitch to pursue."

   "And now…
   Let the Feast of Grumbling begin…"

"Some folks say
Things are looking up,
We say things
Are always looking down.
Things get worse,
Worse from head to toe;
Be prepared for melancholy woe,

Grump, grump, grump,
Grump, grump, grump,
It's our trade
To grump, grump, grump.

We can frown,
The biggest frowns in town,
We can make
The grumpiest of sounds;
We can argue
Every pro and con,
We can feel
The worst of anyone.

Grump, grump, grump,
Grump, grump, grump,
It's our trade
To grump, grump, grump."

70

"Well sung," said Dr. Frump,
"And now…Let the game begin…"

In blue-green tunics, with blue-green mallets,
The Grumps shuffled into position,
  Scuffling and mumbling,
  Gruffling and grumbling,
According to long-time tradition.

"Now, struggle to play together this day,
But not *too* close, mind you," Frump called.
  Then with the first blow,
  A Grump cried, "My toe!
Ouch! Ouch! you hit *me*, not the ball!"

"You got in the way," his partner replied,
"You should have known better, instead."
  "Don't say that word, 'better,'
  My mind it will fetter,
Get Dr. Frump, quick, my toe's red!"

"Glum-double, double, toil and trouble,
Take two sour grapes in a hurry,"
  Said Dr. Frump
  To the injured Grump,
"You're sure to get worse, so don't worry."

71

Colleen M. Scott

Then Frump tipped his head at a sound he heard,
Like the trill of a lilting swallow,
  "What an awful noise,
   It spoils my poise,
Someone singing in Grumpy Hollow?"

Brighter and clearer the singing came,
With happy songs praising and voicing,
  'Twas Smiley Saroo,
   With his oil bottles, too,
On his way to the Feast of Rejoicing!

Dr. Frump frowned his most scowly-frown,
And peered through the thick grumpwood tangle:
  "This is hallowed ground
   For grumping sound,
Not for singing such jingle-jangle!"

"Who are you? You don't belong here,
We don't need your smiles and your song,"
   Dr. Frump scowled,
   Right down to his jowl,
"You've taken a path that is wrong!"

"I am the Smiley Saroo, good friends,
And this is the right kind of place,
   For a Smiley Saroo
   With what's good for you,"
Said Saroo with a twinkling face.

"That face hurts my eyes, that voice hurts my ears,"
Said one Grump right after another.
   "You need a good dose
   Of crabapple juice,
To stop all your jovial bother."

"What do you do with your dreadful self,
And your singing that makes my ears thump?
   It's a serious thing,
   To make the ears ring
Of the Chief of the Grumps—Dr. Frump."

"Well, Dr. Frump, it's a pleasure to tell
Of my calling, and just what I do.
   And now that you ask,
   It's a happy task
Living life as a Smiley Saroo."

73

And before the Grumps could grump again,
The Smiley Saroo twirled his cane;
  With laughter and dance,
  A skip and a prance,
In his song he began to explain:

"When I see folks in any town
Start to grumble, and start to frown,
This funny bird, called "Smiley Saroo,"
Pulls up their lips, and they smile, too.
Now a Smiley Saroo
Has a smile you can catch,
And wherever he goes
People smile by the batch…"

"Stop! Stop! Don't finish!"
  Cried all the Grumps…

"You'll not catch us smiling down here, Saroo,"
Said Frump. "And you're wasting our time;
  Your alien heart,
  Oil bottles and cart,
Are spoiling our Festival's clime."

He called to the Grumps, "Let's sing our own song,
March on!" And they circled the Hollow;
  With notes woebegone,
  The Grumps fumbled on,
Intent in their grumping to wallow.

Plodding around, not one saw the sign
That hung on the front of the cart,
  "Merry hearts do good,
  Like a medicine should,
Oil of Gladness will bring a new heart!"

OIL OF GLADNESS

"Merry Hearts Do Good
Like a Medicine Should.
Oil of Gladness will
Bring a New Heart!"

74

Then Smiley Saroo took some of his oil,
And when the Grumps came to a halt,
   With twinkling eyes,
   He said, "I'll advise
My medicine oil for your fault."

"Here, Dr. Frump, is a remedy you need,
This is just the right medicine for you."
   "Medicine, you say?
   Don't hurry away,
You're now talking our language, Saroo."

"It's a bitter, horrible-tasting stuff,
And of course, no results," Frump said.
   "Well, this kind of oil
   You don't drink at all;
I'll just pour it all over your head!"

"Feels good to look down, Saroo, feels good,"
Agreed Dr. Frump, bending down,
   As out of the spout
   Oil of Gladness poured out
All over his grumpy crown.

"Come on Grumps, in your favorite position,
Bend down, everyone, here by me;
   Hats off, to a man,
   Let's get all that we can
Of this medicine, while it is free."

75

Colleen M Scott

So the Oil of Gladness trickled on down
All the Grumps there in Grumpy Hollow,
  Working its power,
  In joyful shower,
With Saroo knowing all that would follow.

Lightly, then bubbling, and bursting aloud,
The merriment grew and grew;
  With laughter and shouts,
  And dancing about,
All the Grumps skipped round Smiley Saroo!

"A merry heart is good for your health,"
Said Saroo, "and is good for your face;
  A cheerful mind
  Will work wonders, you'll find,
In a wisdom that's not commonplace."

"Today is the Feast of Rejoicing,
Why not join me and all come along."
  "We're no longer Grumps,"
  Replied Dr. Frump,
"And we'll join you right *now* in a song!"

Happily singing, they blew the green mist
Away, and the Hollow turned bright;
  And in perfect key,
  This song, merrily,
Brought in rainbows of golden sunlight:

"If you think a merry heart
    Is good for your health,
All in favor say, 'Aye!'
    If you think God's blessing
Is the greatest of wealth,
    All in favor say, 'Aye!'
If you think a drop of Oil
    Of Gladness will raise
Happy hands of clapping
    That will brighten your days,
If you think that you can sing
    A new song of praise,
    All in favor say...
    All in favor say...
    All in favor say, 'AYE!' "

And the happy Grumps cheered
And said..."AYE! AYE! AYE!"

BOBBING THINGS

Bobbing things are everywhere!
  Duck tails bobbing, by the pair;
Bottles corked upon the sea;
  Apples in a tub, for me!
Robins bobbing on the ground;
  Bobbing things are all around!

Bobbing things are everywhere!
  Land or sea, or in the air;
But the nicest bobbing sight,
  Around the world, and every night,
Is heads-a-bobbing in sweet prayer;
  Yes, bobbing heads are everywhere!

PEAS IN A POD

Peas in a pod, peas in a pod,
Each pea telling words from God!
    First Pea   —Praise!
    Second Pea —Prayer!
    Third Pea   —Power!
    Fourth Pea —Prepare!
    Fifth Pea   —Purpose!
    Sixth Pea   —Prize!
    Seventh Pea —Peace!
Words to the wise!
Peas in a pod, peas in a pod,
Each pea telling words from God!

IF I'D AS MUCH MONEY AS
I COULD SPEND

If I'd as much money as I could spend,
I never a broken heart could mend;
I never could buy the snow to send,
Or buy a trip to the rainbow's end,
If I'd as much money as I could spend.

If I'd as much money as I could tell,
  I never could make a cockle shell;
I never could stay the spring's farewell,
  Or store the tide to buy and sell,
If I'd as much money as I could tell.

If I'd as much money from Pole to Pole,
  I never could buy my friend's dear soul,
For only Jesus can make us whole,
  And write our names on Heaven's scroll;
        And HE ever could!
      Oh, HE ever would
      Do all these things,
      Kindly and free,
      Out of His love
      For you and me.

THE NOOKS AND CRANNIES

In the Nooks and Crannies,
   Live the Gramps and Grannies,
So wise in years and thought;
   All the reams of words
   They have learned and heard,
They sift, and save, and sort.

They are very thrifty,
   And are very swifty
To use words that are the best;
   To select each word
   That is preferred,
They prepare a simple test.

They will chew and savor
   Every word's own flavor,
And their taste buds tell the tale;
   They can tell what's sweet,
   And what's good to eat,
And what's sour, and cross, and stale.

With such fine selection,
    Their condensed collection
Of wisdom is like pure gold;
    Each word is seasoned
    With salt, and reasoned
To be shared with each household.

So the Gramps and Grannies,
    In the Nooks and Crannies,
Arrange words in small lots.
    They write them on scrolls,
    And bake them in rolls,
And store them away in pots.

It is said that some Gramps,
    Who could chew words like champs,
Gained fame by words that were few;
    And a quiet Granny,
    With wisdom uncanny,
Reduced ten words to just two!

For the Gramps and Grannies,
  In the Nooks and Crannies,
Remember short proverbs well;
  And have passed them on down,
  Winning much renown
From wise and good words they tell.

Today they are baking
  The rolls they are taking
To join the Feast, with their friends;
  They'll stuff all the rolls,
  With "good advice" scrolls,
They've practiced, and preached and penned.

The rolls that are rising
  Smell most appetizing,
And Grannies have stuffed them well,
  With, "Birds of a feather
  Flock together,"
And, "Time and tide will tell."

The rolls nearly done,
  Say, "Like father, like son,"
And, "A stitch in time saves nine."
  While those on the shelf
  Are stuffed, "Health is wealth,"
And, "Let your little light shine."

84

The rolls extra crusty,
　　Are filled with words trusty:
"Wisdom is better than gold."
　　And, "A friend in need
　　Is a friend indeed."
"The half has not yet been told!"

In double-roll hollows,
　　A double scroll follows
The shape of the double bun;
　　"Two wrongs don't make right,"
　　Is baked in there, tight,
With, "Two heads are better than one."

A Little Child Shall Lead Them

The rolls Gramps are stacking,
　　And Grannies are packing,
Say, "Love will cover all things."
　　And those on a tray,
　　Being carried away,
Say, "I will trust under His wings."

Now the Gramps and Grannies,
　　From the Nooks and Crannies,
Are off to the Feast, God-speed them!
　　With a cart load of rolls,
　　And a banner with scrolls:
" A little child shall lead them."

85

HOT CROSS BUNS

Hot cross buns,
Hot cross buns,
One a penny,
Two a penny,
Hot cross buns.
Give them to your daughters,
Give them to your sons,
Tell them Who's The Bread of Life!
Hot cross buns.

86

THE NORTH WIND DOTH BLOW

The north wind doth blow,
And we shall have snow,
And what will poor robin do then?
Poor thing.
He'll sit in a barn,
And keep himself warm,
And wait for God's sunshine and spring,
Wise thing!

WHAT IF?

What if?…
We never knew
If we jumped in the air,
Whether we would come down
Right away, or next year!

What if?…
The sun might rise,
And then it might not.
And icicles chilly,
Were sometimes red hot!

What if?…
The rain rained *up*,
And once a year, *down!*
And smiles could get loose,
And turn into frowns!

What if?…
Once in a while
The corn came up peas!
And all of the seeds
Had no guarantees!

What if?…
Suddenly, cows
Gave pink lemonade!
And sometimes the lemons
Grew dark purple shade!

Colleen M. Scott

88

What if?…
The moon might shine,
And then it might not.
And bees made no honey,
Because they forgot!

What if?…
A day at times
Turned two days instead!
And springtime arrived
In December ahead!

What if?…
The tide went out,
But never came in!
And sometimes the earth
Would go for a spin!

But…
Thank you, dear Lord,
You rule earth and space,
And order aright
Everything in its place!

THEODORE T. TOAD III

"Drawbridge down! Let the drawbridge down.
  I'm stepping out today,
Theodore T. Toad the third,
  In grand and glorious array."

"Thank you, Toby, you're now in charge
  Of the halls of Lofty Heights;
I'm off to seek a Mathew Mole,
  And should return by tonight."

So off went Theodore T. Toad
  To Dandelion Sea,
Smartly dressed in spats and vest,
  With a cane held jauntily.

Strutting along the winding path,
　And through the leafy roads,
He sang his favorite walking song,
　"I Am Not As Other Toads."

By ten, he reached the meadow's edge
　At Humpty Dumpty's wall,
And carefully climbed the rocky steps
　So that he would not fall.

"Good morning, Humpty Dumpty, sir;
　How amazing, you're still here!
By legend, you were shattered,
　Now cohesive you appear."

Humpty jumped, and said with a smile,
　"The tale of 'Horses and Men,'
Wasn't the end! The KING HIMSELF,
　Put me together again!"

"Miracles still occur, I'm told,"
　Theodore began to extol,
"But please be so kind to direct me
　To a certain Mathew Mole."

"Keep walking on the meadow path,
　You'll find good help, Mr. Toad,
From neighbors going to the Feast,
　Who'll direct you on the road."

91

Toad saw Mary and her lamb,
   Who were walking up ahead,
With Tommy Tucker pushing mounds
   Of golden barley bread.

They cheerfully directed Toad
   To pass the Old-Shoe House,
Then follow signs near the cottage
   Marked, "Danny D. Dormouse."

Quite soon, Toad reached the little spot
   Where Charlie Cricket lunched;
"Good-day, Mr. Cricket, pardon my
   Intrusion while you munch."

"Is this perchance the rustic road
   To Dandelion Sea?"
Charlie answered, "Indeed, it is.
   You're a stranger here, I see."

"Of course! I live across the moat,
   In splendid Lofty Heights;
I'm Theodore T. Toad the third,
   From a line of titled knights."

"I'm Charlie Cricket, Mr. Toad,
   And the happy mailman here;
Are you related to Stubmie Toad,
   Our surveyor-engineer?"

92

"Please observe, I'm a high-born Toad,
    Well versed in law, and refined;
Such toads as Stubmie Toad can't be
    Related to *my* toads' kind."

"I see, Mr. Toad, quite clearly,
    You're not from these parts at all,
So may I ask what brings you here,
    And to what do we owe your call?"

"I'm seeking out a Mathew Mole,
    Who wears a watch, I hear,
That fits a Lofty Heights heirloom
    That's been lost for many a year."

"Mathew Mole! he's my best friend;
    A gentleman, good and kind.
He's better known as Grandpa Mole,
    The most honest mole you'll find."

"How far then is it to his house?"
    Toad asked, "which is the way?"
Charlie replied, "Follow that sign;
    It's seventy-five hops by survey."

"Seventy-five hops! How far is *that*?
    Such survey sounds quite silly.
Did Stubmie Toad use standards hops,
    Or metric hops, or milli?"

Charlie smiled, "It's not so far;
    I'll take you, if you like."
"No, thank you," Toad said, walking off,
    "I prefer a *private* hike."

93

He rambled on through yellow flowers,
  "Tut-tutting" all the time,
When all at once he heard a voice
  Say, "Children, here's a rhyme."

"Twinkle, twinkle, little star,
God has placed you where you are;
Up above the world so high,
You're God's light hung in the sky."

"Great cackling figments! Mother Goose!"
  He puffed around a bend,
Seeing Mother Goose upon a log
  Reciting to her friends.

"Madam, what pure simplicity;
  Such unscholastic bliss.
The minds of children should be primed
  By versions such as this:

"Scintillate, scintillate,
Stellar diminutive;
Deity hath established
Thine abode, definitive.
Pre-eminently poised
Aloft terrestrial,
Deity's illumination
Suspended—celestial!"

94

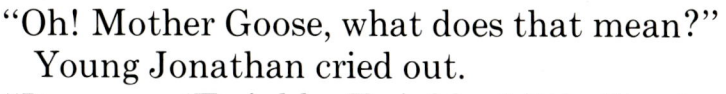

"Oh! Mother Goose, what does that mean?"
 Young Jonathan cried out.
"It means, 'Twinkle, Twinkle, Little Star,'
 With the words turned inside-out."

"My version quite escapes the minds
 Of this fair wonderland,"
Theodore said, "but I commend
 Its friendly, helping hands."

"I'm on my way to Mathew Mole
 Who lives around this section;
Please inform me if I'm correct
 In taking this direction."

"We're meeting Grandpa Mole quite soon,
 For our special Feast today,"
Mother Goose smiled. "Perhaps you'd like
 To join us on the way."

"A special Feast? And what about?"
 Theodore asked in surprise.
"A Feast to rejoice in God's great love,"
 Little Jane, with smiles, replied.

"What quaint traditions you have here
 In Dandelion Sea,"
Theodore sighed, "but I extend
 My thanks for inviting me."

"Goodbye, Mother Goose and children,"
 Then strutting off once more,
Theodore and his walking song
 Performed a fine encore.

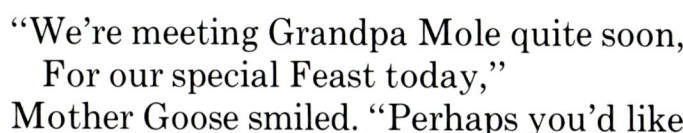

Arriving at the meadow's edge,
   He spied Mole's house beyond;
"Ah-hah! I've found you, watch and all,"
   He called across the pond.

Just as he knocked at Mole's front door,
   He heard a chuckling voice,
Singing somewhere from underground,
   "Sorrabahum!" and "Rejoice!"

Theodore crept to the hole nearby,
   Where the singing swirled about;
And peering in, came face to face
   With Mole who was coming out!

GRANDPA MOLE

Their noses touched, meeting eye to eye,
   "Mathew Mole, sir, I presume.
I'm Theodore T. Toad the third."
   Grandpa Mole said, "Sorrabahum!"

"Sorrabahum? Now, what is that?
   A local word, no doubt."
"That's how a mole says, 'Bless you,' "
   Grandpa Mole said, climbing out.

Putting down his juice for the Feast,
   Mole smiled, "Now, years ago,
My grandfather knew *your* grandfather,
   Our family records show."

96

"*My* grandfather knew *your* grandfather!
　　That's not our custom today.
You live in a hole, Mr. Mole;
　　A mansion's my home, by the way."

Mole quietly quoted: "It's better
　　To dwell in a hole in the ground,
Where there's love,
　　Than to dwell in a mansion
Where love and contentment's not found."

"Oh, dear, what quaint little proverbs
　　You people know in these parts,"
Theodore said. "Now my mission
　　I'd like to conclude, then depart."

"The gold watch you're wearing, Mr. Mole,
　　Belongs in *our* collection;
A fine antique—missing many years—
　　That was lost in Boat-Bay section."

"That's where my grandfather found this watch!
　　And passed it down with care;
Most ordinary moles never have
　　Such a fine, gold watch to wear."

"I'm prepared to give you, Mr. Mole,
　　Five hundred coins to buy back
This priceless heirloom," Theodore said,
　　While jingling the gold in a sack.

"I cannot accept all your money,"
　　Grandpa Mole, with tears, replied;
As sadly he took off the heirloom
　　He'd worn twenty years with pride.

"Mr. Toad, I have just one request;
   Going home, kindly stop and read
The message engraved inside that watch,
   That must be your family's creed."

"I give you my word, Mr. Mole,
   Since you have been honest and fair,
That on the way home I will ponder
   The message my family left there."

"Goodbye, Mr. Mole, and I thank you."
   "Goodbye, Mr. Toad, I'll now leave
For the Feast of Rejoicing—but somehow—
   This will all work for good, I believe."

So Toad walked back through the meadow,
   Success now quickened his pace;
Rubbing and shining the fine gold watch,
   Till he stopped to open the case.

Only five words were engraved there,
   But those words gave Toad a shock;
He read, "Love thy neighbor as thyself,"
   Then gasped, and fell over a rock!

The fine gold watch flew through the air,
   And Theodore landed in pain;
"Help! Help, someone! Oh, my ankle;
   I've suffered an awful sprain!"

98

Charlie Cricket came running by,
    And said, "What happened to you?"
"I tripped and stumbled on that rock,"
    Moaned Theodore, black and blue.

"The *best* of toads can take a fall,"
    Wise Charlie gently spoke;
"I'll see that you get into town
    For help from friendly folk."

Then Charlie helped Theodore get up,
    And hobbling off together,
Theodore's pain made him forget
    The watch—in a clump of heather!

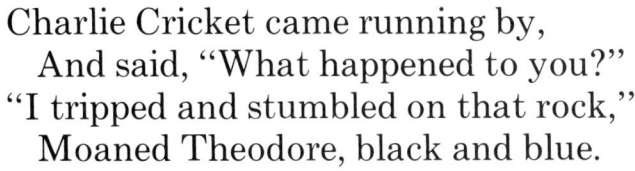

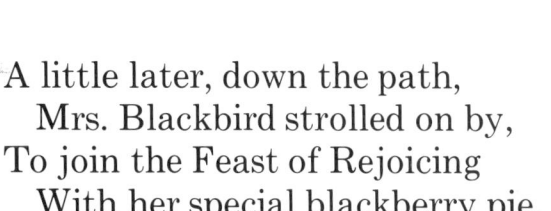

A little later, down the path,
    Mrs. Blackbird strolled on by,
To join the Feast of Rejoicing
    With her special blackberry pie.

Her keen eyes saw the fine gold watch;
    "That's Grandpa Mole's!" she cried.
"He must have lost it—I'll take it back."
    So she ran with longer stride.

Then Mrs. Blackbird, watch, and pie,
    Went on to meet her friends,
Quite unaware she plays a part
    In how this story ends.

But, oh, it's the Feast of Rejoicing!
    When things should be made right.
Be very sure, we'll meet Mr. Toad,
    Grandpa Mole, and the watch before night.

99

HEY DIDDLE DINKETY,
POPPETY, PET

Hey diddle dinkety, poppety, pet,
    The merchants of London
Have formed a quartet!
    Wearing their garments
Of praise, hat to hem,
    So merrily sing the merchant men!

THE RAIN FOREST

The rain forest is
 The most pleasant place yet,
Especially for creatures
 Who like to get wet.

And even the ones
 Who like to stay dry,
Will drop in to see
 What goes on passing by.

The rain that falls there
 Is not usual rain;
When it falls, things will happen
 No one can explain.

Nothing-Impossible-Possum
 Lives near,
And watches for signs
 Of the rain to appear.

One of the signs
 Is a great weather vane,
That spins seven times
 At the coming of rain!

Nothing-Impossible-Possum
 Can tell
Wonderful tales,
 Of the forest's wet spell.

101

For the rain forest clouds
  Are not dark and drear,
But hold rainbow-rain
  That drops crystally-clear.

Nothing-Impossible-Possum
  Looks out,
To keep careful watch
  As a rainbow-rain scout.

The moment he sees
  The weather vane spin,
He blows on his flute
  A quick news bulletin.

RAIN
FOREST
WATCH FOR FORMER AND LATTER RAINS
♥ BLESSINGS WHEN WET ♥
NOTHING-IMPOSSIBLE-POSSUM, RAINBOW RAIN SCOUT
BY APPOINTMENT OF HIS MAJESTY

"The rain is coming,
  The rainbow-rain!
Leave what you're doing,
  Don't stop to explain.

Bring all the children!
  Such wonders to see,
Out in the rain
  'Neath a rain forest tree."

Then down comes the rain!
  And through each lovely drop,
Your eyes can see under,
  Instead of on top!

Inside of tree trunks,
  Right down to the root,
You'll see little seeds
  Dressing up to be fruit!

You can see how the soil
  Drinks up the soft rain,
To help push up flowers,
  And long stalks of grain.

The small clumps of herbs,
  At the first drops that fall,
Sprout into a garden
  Exceedingly tall!

The rain magnifies
  Everything you see in it;
That's why you can see
  The whole land in a minute!

Nothing-Impossible-Possum
  Said he
Saw small drops of rain
  That turned into a sea!

Then saw the great sea
  Become a great ocean,
From little rain showers
  Joined merry, in motion.

Nothing-Impossible-Possum's
  In tune
With the news of the greatest
  Of rains—coming soon!

And what will it bring?
  Well, it's written, no doubt;
So watch for the bright clouds
  To rain, and find out!

I SAW A SHIP A-SAILING

I saw a ship a-sailing,
  A-sailing on the sea;
And, oh, but it was laden
  With happy gifts for Thee!

There was singing in the cabin,
  And praising in the hold;
The sails were made of linen,
  And the masts were made of gold.

There were gifts in little boxes,
  And gifts in treasure chests;
Candlesticks and apples,
  With spices—just the best!

104

And precious little vessels
    Were neatly packed aboard;
The flags were flying high,
    "Cheery Givers to The Lord!"

The decks were filled with children,
    A-sailing off so brave;
And tanks of thanks were bobbing
    Up and down with every wave.

The captain was a father,
    A gallant, cheery chap;
And when the ship began to move
    The children cheered and clapped!

THEODORE T. TOAD RETURNS

The table is all ready
   In Polly-Woggle Park,
Brother Rabbit will be host,
   From afternoon to dark.

Grandpa Mole is helping him
   To set the juice in place;
Everyone will soon arrive,
   And greet with fond embrace.

For all of Dandelion Sea
   Looks forward, once a year,
To meeting friends on Feast Day,
   In God's love and friendship dear.

Brother Rabbit checked the time;
   "I'll miss your watch," he said
To Grandpa Mole, who nodded,
   "Well, it's Theodore's now, instead."

"That watch will soon be hanging
   In the halls of Lofty Heights,
And rightly so, it came from there,
   And should be back tonight."

"I see the first arrivals
   Coming down the meadow road,"
Brother Rabbit looked—then cried,
   "Oh dear, it's Mr. Toad!"

Theodore came with limp and groan,
   On Charlie Cricket's shoulder;
"I fell, while looking in that watch;
   My ankle struck a boulder."

106

Grandpa Mole said, "Sit right here,
    We'll bandage up the sprain,
And help you get back safely
    With your watch, back home again."

"The watch, the watch, I've lost it!"
    Theodore suddenly realized.
"I hurt so much I quite forgot
    My priceless, heirloom prize."

"How sad, but we'll help find it,"
    Grandpa Mole assured poor Toad,
As Mrs. Blackbird rushed to them
    With, "See my precious load?"

"Grandpa Mole, I found your watch
    Along the meadow road."
"Thank you, but that watch belongs
    To Theodore T. Toad."

"How kind and honest, Madam,
    To return it," Theodore spoke;
"But far more precious is my foot,
    And help from kindly folk."

"We'll gather willing hands,"
    Grandpa Mole said, cheerily,
"To get you back to Lofty Heights;
    Stay! Share the Feast with me."

"Grandpa Mole, your kind request
    I do accept herein,"
Said Theodore, settling on a log,
    To watch the Feast begin.

And that's how Mr. Toad became
    The unexpected guest,
At Polly-Woggle Park that day,
    Which changed things for the best.

THE FEAST
AT POLLY-WOGGLE PARK

Wee Willie Winkie's band is in tune,
For the Feast of Rejoicing afternoon.
Everyone's coming, from here and from there;
Everyone's bringing a gift to share.

Barley bread, honey, and rolls stuffed with scrolls;
Chunky cheese; apples in bright-colored bowls.
Garden peas, parsley, and walnuts and thyme;
Wee, smiling children are bringing a rhyme!

Hear Brother Rabbit address the fine crowd;
Hear what he's saying so joyfully loud:

"Our table's prepared to dine together;
Rejoice in God's love, old or young; all weather!
Praise Him with singing; praise Him with prayer;
Praise Him with laughter; with breath everywhere!
Hear the trees clapping; hear the hills sing!
Rejoice every creature! Let thanksgiving ring!"

Happy, small creatures in this pleasant land,
Cheered Brother Rabbit with clapping of hands,
But off to the side, one thoughtful face showed
His heart had been touched—Theodore T. Toad!
Theodore then whispered in Mother Goose's ear;
She smiled with delight at such kind words to hear.

Then taking his watch, and holding it high,
She announced to all, "It's with pleasure that I
Present this gift to the Feast celebration,
From Theodore T. Toad's entire generation.
The watch he has given to grace the household
Of our friend and counselor, Grandpa Mole!"

Everyone cheered with, "Hip, hip, hurray!"
And the band joined in with a trumpet display;
Till the whole land rang with the cheery voicing,
On the wonderful day of the Feast of Rejoicing!

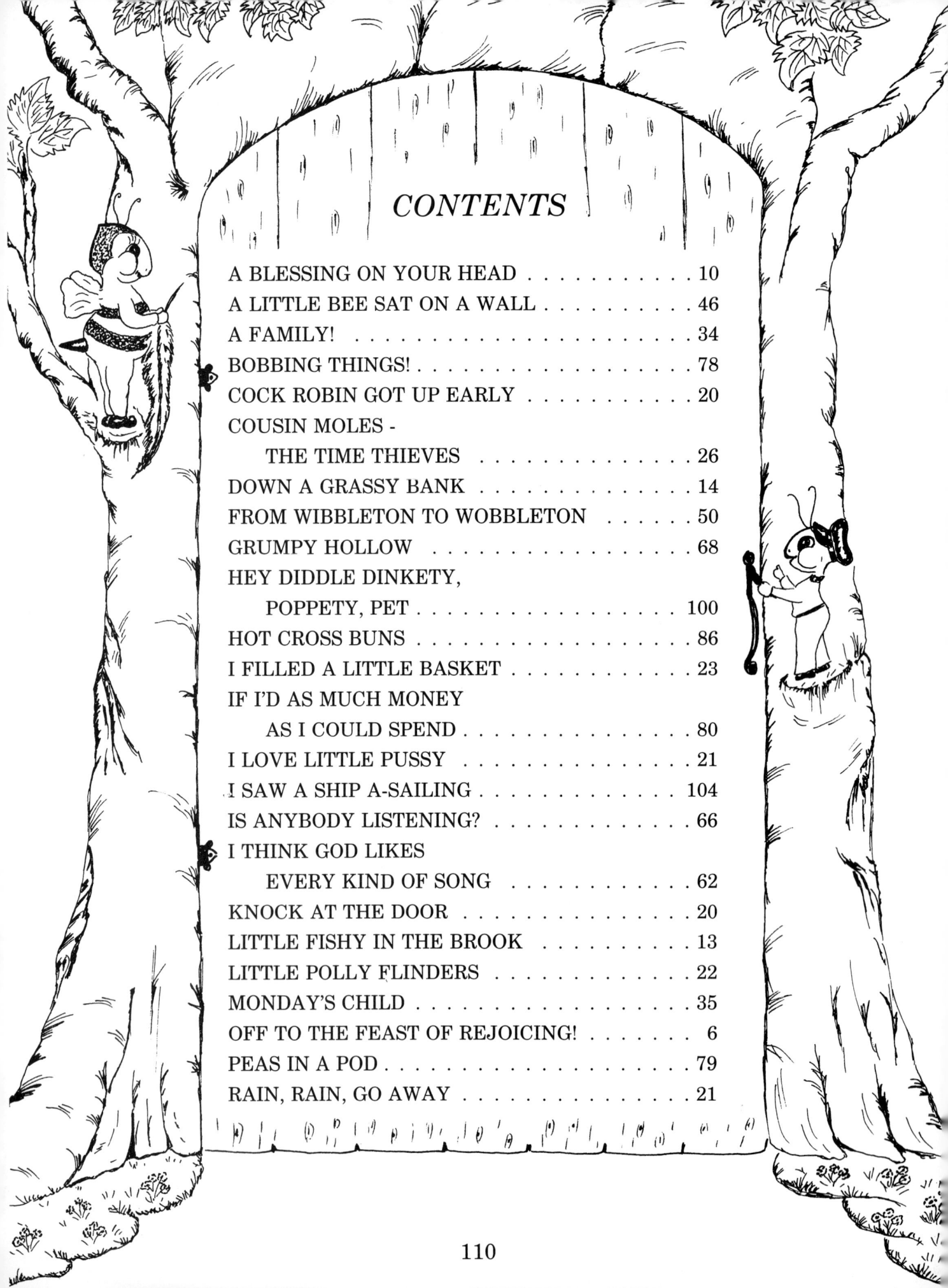

CONTENTS

A BLESSING ON YOUR HEAD 10

A LITTLE BEE SAT ON A WALL 46

A FAMILY! 34

BOBBING THINGS! 78

COCK ROBIN GOT UP EARLY 20

COUSIN MOLES -
    THE TIME THIEVES 26

DOWN A GRASSY BANK 14

FROM WIBBLETON TO WOBBLETON 50

GRUMPY HOLLOW 68

HEY DIDDLE DINKETY,
    POPPETY, PET 100

HOT CROSS BUNS 86

I FILLED A LITTLE BASKET 23

IF I'D AS MUCH MONEY
    AS I COULD SPEND 80

I LOVE LITTLE PUSSY 21

I SAW A SHIP A-SAILING 104

IS ANYBODY LISTENING? 66

I THINK GOD LIKES
    EVERY KIND OF SONG 62

KNOCK AT THE DOOR 20

LITTLE FISHY IN THE BROOK 13

LITTLE POLLY FLINDERS 22

MONDAY'S CHILD 35

OFF TO THE FEAST OF REJOICING! 6

PEAS IN A POD 79

RAIN, RAIN, GO AWAY 21

RING-A-RING-O'ROSES 11

SIX LITTLE MICE

    SAT DOWN TO SPIN 64

SOMEBODY! 22

THE BEST TOUCH OF ALL 25

THE CHIMNEY SWEEP FLIGHT 56

THE FEAST AT

    POLLY-WOGGLE PARK 108

THE FIVE COBBLERS 36

THEODORE T. TOAD III 90

THEODORE T. TOAD RETURNS 106

THE NOOKS AND CRANNIES 82

THE NORTH WIND DOTH BLOW 87

THE RAIN FOREST 101

THIS IS THE WAY 24

THREE LITTLE KITTENS 12

WHAT IF? 88

WHERE ARE YOU GOING TO,

    MY PRETTY MAID? 48

YOU MADE THE MONTHS FOR ME 52

"... A Little Child Shall Lead Them."

ABOUT THE AUTHOR . . .

Best-Seller author, Marjorie Ainsborough Decker, is originally from Liverpool, England. As author, playwright and well-loved speaker, she has an extensive ministry in the U.S.A. and overseas.

Marjorie is a recognized student of the Word. She brings fresh enthusiasm and dynamic faith to biblical scholarship. Her reputation as a popular Bible teacher has earned many invitations as a featured speaker at seminars, banquets and convocations. Genuinely committed to the Gospel of The Lord Jesus Christ, Mrs. Decker brings the love of God and His message to every age and situation. She speaks with authority and credits God with giving her something to share.